The Keys to Life
Volume 1

Derrick E. Drisdel

D1603386

Zanzara Press
an imprint of
Culicidae Press

Zanzara Press
918 5TH ST
Ames, IA 50010
USA
zanzarapress.com
editor@zanzarapress.com

Zanzara Press
an imprint of
Culicidae Press

THE KEYS TO LIFE, VOLUME 1
2022 © by Derrick E. Drisdel

ISBN-13: 978-1-941892-56-5

Edited by Mikesch Muecke
Book layout and design by polytekton.com

Dedication

For Monica, Jonathan, Casey, Cedrick,
Jade, Sparkle, and Cheri

I hope the words in this book will stay with you
and serve as a guide as you travel through life.

Your father Derrick Ethan Drisdel, aka Daddy D

Introduction

This book is called *The Keys to Life*. I received the first Key to Life from my father when I was about eight years old. My father was a bus driver then, and during that time bus drivers used a change maker in order to make change for the passengers. That's why my father always had a lot of change lying around the house. I remember one summer day, when I asked my father if he had any extra money, so I could go to the store and buy a popsicle. That's when he said: "There is no such thing as extra money." I didn't know it at the time but that became my first Key to Life. As I grew older, I can recall several other Keys of Life given to me by my father. Sometimes he would tell me: "You may not understand right now but when the situation presents itself, you will remember these words."

I remember being in college, calling my father long distance, and telling him: "Hey Pop, I remember a long time ago you told me such and such; man, it just happened, and I'm glad I knew what to do at the time." Sometimes he would drop a Key on me without any situation occurring. For instance, I remember one day he said to me: "Rick, if you want to have a good life, just be good." I said: "That's it?" and he said: "Yeah, it's so simple it's like a secret, because most people aren't doing it." I would always scratch my head and say: "Wow, that's deep." As time went on, I began to develop my own Keys to Life. Some would come to me through life experiences, and some I would create by watching other people's experiences.

The Keys that I learned from my father and through life experiences were so valuable, I began sharing them with my children. At one point I was sharing some of the Keys to Life with my kids till one of them said to me: "Wow, Pop, that's clever. Why don't you put all this down in a book?" I said: "That's a good idea!" And before long I started to write this book called *The Keys to Life*. I'm sure we all have looked back and said to ourselves: "I wish I knew, when I was younger, what I know now. I would have done things differently."

I hope that as you read these *Keys to Life*, they will give you an objective approach to situations that may occur in your life, and that they someday open doors to you that would normally be closed. My hope is that, as you read this book, you open your mind, think about the information being shared, and develop an objective approach to some of life's challenges. If you use these Keys, I guarantee you that they will help you free your mind. And if I may quote my former boss George Clinton: "Free your mind and your behind will follow." I told my kids: "If you find *The Keys to Life* helpful…it's already a success."

The Keys to Life

The first and perhaps most important key to life is: God sometimes places obstacles in our path to make us stronger, but he also gives us the means and the devices to overcome them.

You have already made it through
100% of all your bad days.

A winner goes through a problem. A loser tries unsuccessfully to go around it.

If you live to be 60 and you sleep
8 hours a day you would have slept
for 20 years or ⅓ of your life.

When you attempt to cover up a
lie with unnecessary details you
make the lie more visible.

Don't waste time thinking
about wasted time.

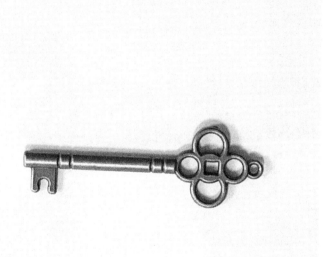

Time is so important, they invented
a device to go on your wrist so
you can keep up with it.

There is no such thing as extra time.

Being on time requires preparation.

Experience gives you the test
and then the lesson.

Your quality of life depends on the decisions you make all day every day for the rest of your life.

Alcohol and drugs have the ability
to rob you of your ambition.

After you get high...you get low.

Excuses give you permission to come up short, and even fail.

Being bad blocks blessings.

Learn from, and follow, good examples.

The time you have left is more important than the time you have already used.

The best way to receive respect is to give it.

If you are looking for the perfect mate, you must be perfect yourself; it's not going to happen.

Anger hurts the host the most.

God will not give you the test without
giving you the tools to pass.

God feeds every bird on the planet
every day, but he does not take the
food and place it in their nest.

God cannot make you stronger until
you lift some spiritual weights.

You can change the future if you
are willing to let go of the past.

When you let go of who you
think you are, you make room for
who you were meant to be.

Tired minds do not plan well.

When you stress, you're using the energy
that it takes to fix the problem.

If you deal in truth the good part
of you will reject the bad part.

Sometimes it takes a long
time to be like yourself.

Life is not short, but it is the
longest thing you will ever do.

Don't make the same
mistakes as your father.

You have to show yourself love
before expecting it from others.

Sometimes you have to relearn
things that you already know.

You won't be late if you leave early
enough to allow for mishaps.

Sometimes you have to remind
yourself to be happy.

There is no such thing as (almost)
it either did or didn't happen.

When you lose, don't lose the lesson.

Before you change your condition,
you must first change yourself.

Never get a habit that can't
be kept up with.

Always have a daily, weekly,
and monthly agenda.

Don't wait for six strong men to
bring you into the church.

Don't let the little things in life get you down (they're all little things).

Everything you do can be improved.

Complaining is a form of
mental destruction.

Hope and fear cannot occupy the same space in your mind. You must choose one or the other.

You must do what you can,
until you can do better.

Don't be affected by receiving
less than what you give.

The best way to honor your father
is to raise good children.

It is easier to raise good children
than it is to fix broken men.

If you want to have a good life, just be good (it's so simple, it's like a secret).

Every life comes with its own personal map. All you have to do is recognize and follow the signs (stop, go, U-turn, caution, etc.).

If someone will lie to you,
they will lie about you.

Don't save the best for last; you may only get one shot. First impressions are important.

You must keep your anger short;
if you don't it may take you down
to a level that is unhealthy.

Stumbling is not falling.

Every day is a good day because
God only gives you so many.

Always try one more time.

The future belongs to those
who believe in dreams.

If you can't find happiness, then make it.

You can't solve all problems with money or power. Sometimes it requires a change of heart.

If you have a brain in your head,
and feet in your shoes, you can go
in any direction you choose.

You must learn to be as patient as a statue. It will add to your character.

Say 'thank you' as often as you can. It will make a big difference in the way you are treated and respected.

The most important time in
your life? It's not the past, it's not
the future, it's right now.

You only live once is not true.
You live every time you wake
up. You only die once.

It's good to be good and
it's right to be right.

If you don't start each day asking yourself, what can you do to make your life better, then you're wasting it.

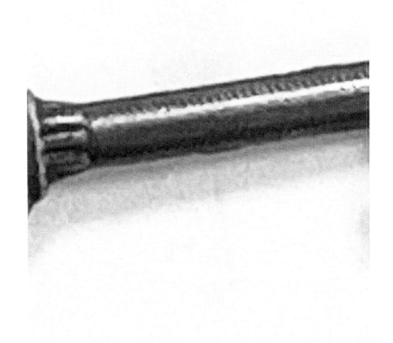

Be kind to everyone and doors will open up for you as you travel through life.

The one person you should never lie to is the person in the mirror.

If you know you're right,
then stop arguing!

Give a man a fish and he can eat
for that day. Teach him how to
fish and he can eat every day.

You should work as long as you can,
and money has nothing to do with it.

The loudest one in the room is usually the weakest one in the room.

Good memories will increase your
health and extend your life.

Laugh at least once a day and three things will happen: 1. You feel better. 2. You will have a better day, and 3. You will live longer.

It's not about how many times
you get knocked down, it's about
how many times you get up.

Hard work beats talent, when
talent doesn't work hard.

Nothing comes to stay,
everything comes to pass.

Pride will deprive you.

The price of success is hard work.

You must always keep a positive attitude.

You won't be measured by what you have.
You'll be measured by what you give.

A man can't ride your back
unless it is bent.

When you are kind to your enemies,
you rob them of their weapons.

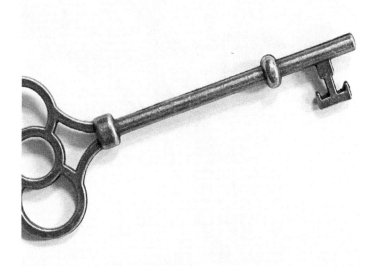

You can change the future if you are
willing to put the past behind you.

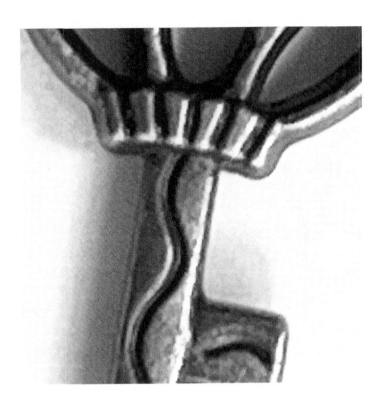

People who are optimists find
opportunity in difficult situations;
people who are pessimists find difficulty
in situations of opportunity.

Don't find the problem to the solution.

Once your mind is made up, it
destroys fear and doubt.

You must show yourself love before
you receive it from others.

You miss out on every opportunity
that you don't take advantage of.

It's not about what you do when people are watching. It's about what you do when no one is watching.

The fear of failure leads to no success.

As soon as you quit a bad habit,
you will like yourself better.

It is so important to be kind to everyone you meet. It shapes your character.

Success demands a greater effort.

In real life there is no yesterday, today, and tomorrow. It is all one continuous long journey.

If everything is perfect, there is no opportunity to grow.

Say less and do more.

God is everywhere you are.

There is a big difference
between hope and faith.

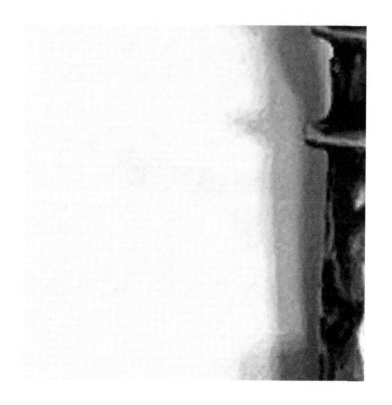

Practice the law of non-resistance.

Do not seek recognition for a job well done. It will come automatically.

Whether you like it or not, part of your job on this earth is to make mistakes so you can warn and prepare your children.

Listen to music you like at least
once a day. It's free medicine.

Positive thought is an energy.

God will not talk to you until
you first talk to him.

The best way to raise good children is
to be truthful and set a good example.

Always reflect on your highlights.

Enjoying yourself is a medicine.

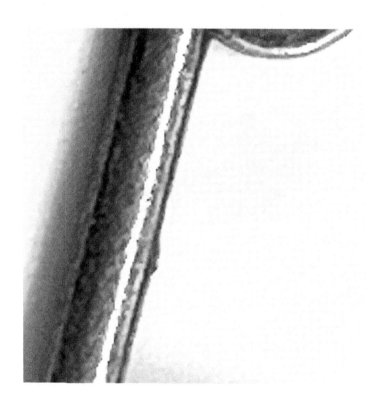

Some of the best things you find in life
are things that you are not looking for.

Take time to think before you react.

If you are a giver, you must have
limits, because a taker has no limits.

Sometimes you have to remind
yourself to be happy.

The thoughts you go to sleep with
grow inside you while you are asleep.

Before you change your condition,
you must first change yourself.

Don't work on the bad habit.
Work on losing the desire.

Being a leader not only requires ability
but it also requires responsibility.

Be careful; it's easy to lie to
yourself because there's no one
around to put you in check.

Exercise and increase your potential.

Don't let anyone make you angry enough to use an excuse to resort back to old bad habits.

Tension and relaxation cannot
fit in the same soul.

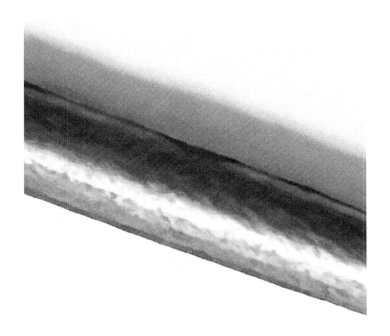

Complaining always makes you feel worse.

The smarter you become, the less you need to speak.

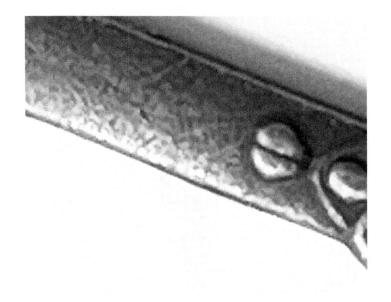

It's not the wrong you do that gets you in trouble; it's the consequences you must face.

Aging is not lost youth. It's
the next stage of life.

Limit your "always" and your "nevers."

There are two parents you can't argue with: Mother Nature and Father Time.

Faith is hope that comes alive.

Who we have in our life is more
important than what we have.

People don't fail, they just stop trying.

It is disappointing to fail but it is more disappointing to not even try.

He that knows patience knows peace.

Don't let yesterday take up
too much of today.

No expectations mean no disappointments.

Leap and the net will appear.

The world is a canvas for your imagination.

Power without love is reckless.

Don't fear storms. Learn
how to sail your ship.

How much you make, is not important;
it's what you do with it that counts.

If you want to go fast, go alone; if you want to go far, go together.

You must do good before you do well.

The best way to avoid confrontation
is to not respond.

Most of the good that you do in life
most people will never know, and if you
are sincere it doesn't matter to you.

Success stands on the shoulders
of many failures.

Hurt people hurt others.

Don't criticize others for their faults, work on your own.

It's important to start; it's more important to finish.

You must learn how to deal
with misfortune.

Remember the devil's job is to distract you from doing the right thing by using temptation.

Being untrustworthy rocks the
foundation of a relationship. It's
no longer earthquake proof

Sometimes silence is the biggest noise.

Success comes from your ability to
take advantage of opportunities.

Luck favors the prepared individual.

The journey is more important
than the destination.

A winner listens. A loser waits
for his turn to talk.

We make a living by what we make.
We make a life by what we give.

Say goodbye to bad habits and
you like yourself better.

If you don't begin each day by saying to yourself "what can I do to make myself better?" you are wasting your life.

Destiny is for those who
refuse to accept failure.

Life is not a problem to be solved.
It's a reality to be experienced.

Work as long as you can. Money
has little to do with it.

Good memories will extend your
life and increase your health.

Money is only good when you use it.

Time is more important than
health and money. You can lose
and regain health. You can
lose and regain money. But once
you lose time...it's gone!

Positive energy works; that's
why they call it energy.

Punctuality says a great deal
about your character.

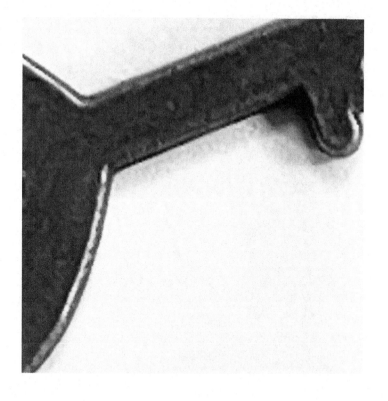

The best way to get respect is to give it.

The one person you should always be able to depend on is that person in the mirror.

Kindness is a language that a blind man
can see and a deaf man can hear.

Faith is belief over doubt.

Being reliable strengthens relationships.

Be kind to all people and you
will be liked by most, and doors
will open for you as you
travel through life.

The lion with the most scars fights the best.

Happiness depends on your
ability to adjust.

There are 86400 seconds in a day; it only takes one second to give thanks.

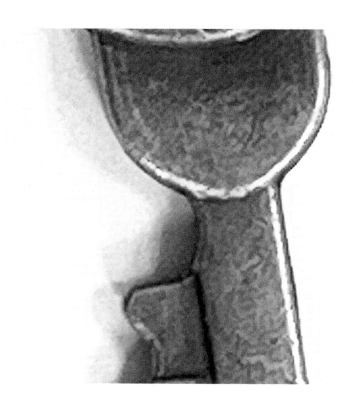

Tough times don't last, but
tough people do.

Dare to let your dreams reach beyond you.

A good cowboy never shoots his last bullet.

You don't ever own anything.
God just allows you to use it for
a certain amount of time.

A happy relationship depends
on your ability to adjust.

In order to exercise your life fully
you must always have plans.

Struggles in life are what helps shape
you into who you will become.

Don't just survive, thrive.

Don't let a lack of tools prevent you from building; you must use what you have.

It's good to be good and
it's right to be right.

Faith sees better in the dark.

Listen and learn from those who are older and more experienced; not because they are always right, but because they have already made the mistakes.

Don't take revenge, because rotten fruit will fall off the tree by itself.

Sometimes it's easier to adjust than fight.

Stop complaining and start counting.

To not stress is a freedom.

Repetition is the father of learning.

Setbacks produce opportunities
to step forward.

True love is sacred.

You must become organized
before you become successful.

Youth gain wisdom by engaging
in things that matter.

Being angry is a pain that we decide
to put ourselves through.

There is no such thing as extra money.

Don't let anyone or anything take away your ability or desire to laugh or smile.

About the Author

Derrick Drisdel was born in 1950 in St. Louis, Missouri, and grew up in East St. Louis, Illinois. He attended Lincoln Senior High, the same high school as famous trumpet player Miles Davis. After moving to Los Angeles, and spending time in the army, he attended  Southwest Junior College, followed by Citrus Junior College, and later graduated from Azusa Pacific University where he played football and basketball.

Derrick began working when he was ten years old, and he has held nearly 100 jobs in his life. His worst two jobs were washing dishes and hanging up hangers in a department store. His two best jobs were teaching school in Monrovia, California, and being Road Manager for George Clinton and Parliament Funkadelic.

Derrick has traveled to more than fifty countries. He is the father of four wonderful children and three fantastic stepchildren, all of whom are professionals in their own right. Their jobs range from police officer to a college volleyball coach. Derrick is happily married to Carla Lindsay Drisdel and he is a saved child of God.

58583382R00118